know your
GUINEA PIGS

by William Ritter

Earl Schneider, editor

THE PET LIBRARY LTD

THE PET LIBRARY LTD ®

Sternco ®

The Pet Library Ltd, sub-
sidiary of Sternco Indus-
tries, Inc., 600 South
Fourth Street, Harrison,
N.J. Exclusive Canadian
Distributor: Hartz Moun-
tain Pet Supplies Limited,
1125 Talbot Street, St.
Thomas, Ontario, Canada.

Exclusive United Kingdom
Distributor: The Pet Library
(London) Ltd, 30 Borough
High Street, London S.E.1.

PRINTED IN THE NETHERLANDS

1 1 3 4 5 6 7 8 9 10

ISBN 0-87826-753-0

CONTENTS

Cover: TOM CARAVAGLIA
Pictures on pages:
5, 8, 9, 12, 17, 28, 32,
33, 40, 44, 52, 53, 56,
57, 60

WILLIAM RITTER

Where it all began—the wild Cavy.

1 What is a Cavy ?

There's something wonderfully endearing about a small furry animal, and the Cavy—you probably know him by his other name, guinea pig—is one of the gentlest and most lovable creatures around. When fully grown, he'll be eight to ten inches long, about four inches high, and will weigh in at from one to three pounds: exactly the right size for hugging (which will suit him just fine, by the way—he loves being petted and scratched). His short brick-shaped body and little limbs weren't made for climbing or jumping, but he doesn't seem to mind. There's plenty to investigate right where he is, and his blunt Roman nose will probably be quivering with curiosity as you offer him a choice carrot top, while his short hairless ears droop forward toward large, clear, prominent eyes. His pointed incisor teeth immediately identify him as a rodent, but he has one very distinctive characteristic, or rather, one distinctly *missing* characteristic: he has no external tail. One of the standard jokes of Cavy breeders is to warn a beginner, "Don't pick a guinea pig up by its tail, or its eyes will fall out." Needless to say, the victim looks quite sheepish when he can't find a tail.

The Cavy's popularity is well-founded. Since Cavies are small, relatively little space is needed to house them, and they require only a minimum of care to keep them healthy and happy. Because of their size and modest needs, it's actually just as easy to have a colony of Cavies as it is to have one. Cavies are usually kept in pairs or in families of one male and two or more females. They don't breed as often as other small rodents do, and their litters are considerably smaller. They come in a wide and delightful variety of colors and hair types, and offer the amateur and professional breeder alike a rewarding challenge. Their disposition is almost invariably gentle and friendly, and many experts affirm that they seldom if ever bite. When kept clean, Cavies are odorless, and if cared for properly, they'll present a clean bill of health over a long life span. Many owners have enjoyed the affectionate companionship of the Cavy for more than seven years.

Guinea pig or Cavy?

No one really seems to know just how our furry friend the Cavy got tagged with the name "guinea pig." We know that he didn't come from the West African coast of Guinea or from New Guinea in the South Pacific. It is true, however, that the ships carrying Cavies from South America came by way of the coast of Guinea, and this may have led people to believe that they came from Guinea rather than from South America.

Another—more plausible—suggestion is that since many Cavies were exported from Guiana in South America, people may have confused the name Guiana with Guinea and used the more familiar Guinea.

The second half of the name is equally misleading, as the Cavy is not even distantly related to the pig. It may have been his general body shape that inspired the name, or the fact (pointed out by one zoologist) that Cavies' flesh is said to be similar to pork in taste. Finally, some animal experts describe the sound the Cavy makes as an "oink." Others, however, insist it is "cui," and still others say it can only be called a squeak or whistle.

Once a name is as widely known as "guinea pig," it's not so easy to change. And to further confuse the issue, adult male Cavies are

English Cavy—Lilac.

Abyssinian Cavy—Black.

English Cavy—Red.

Peruvian Cavy—Chocolate and white.

correctly referred to as boars, and females as sows. But our pet's other name, Cavy (from the genus name *Cavia*) is undoubtedly the more accurate of the two, and we'll use it throughout this book.

Natural history of the Cavy

Cavies were being domesticated in great numbers by the Indians of Peru, Colombia and Ecuador long before Spain conquered the Inca Empire in the sixteenth century. Remains of the Cavy have been found buried together with the mummies in the tombs of the Incas. The Indians kept the Cavy for its meat, which was an important source of nutrition for them. Even today, relatives of these early Cavies are used as sacrificial animals by certain Indian tribes in South America, where wild Cavies can be found in swamps, rocky areas, savannahs and the edges of forests from Colombia and Venezuela down to Brazil and northern Argentina.

When the Swiss explorer J. S. Tschudi traveled across Peru about the middle of the nineteenth century, he came across Cavies in the Indians' huts, where they "ran over the faces of the sleeping inhabitants all night long."

Cavies were introduced to Europe at an early date by the Spaniards returning from their conquests in South America, and there are records dating as far back as 1564 of the "Indian Hare or Piglet"—"Indian" because Columbus had been convinced he had discovered a part of India. The Spanish name for the Cavy, in fact, is "Indian rabbit"—*conejillo de Indias*.

Wild Cavies have often had to struggle bitterly for survival, living off occasional grasses and the flesh of cacti. They only eat a little at a time, and their diet is high in cellulose content, so they have smaller stomachs and intestines than the well-nourished domestic Cavies we know in Europe and North America. The domesticated Cavy, *Cavia porcellus*, is also distinguished from its wild cousins, *Cavia cutlera* and *Cavia tschudi*, by its rounder, plumper head and body. But the most important difference between the wild and domestic Cavy is the exceptionally wide variety in coat type and color found among "our" Cavies. Like the Tin Lizzie Ford, the ancestral Cavy only came in one model, a drab coat of muddy, grizzled fur. By the time the first Cavies came to Europe, however, a red, white and black variety had appeared, and finally—around 1880 or 1890—the Self (solid) colors began to emerge, followed by the agouti. Ironically enough, the grizzled fur of the agouti seems to echo that of the original Cavy, though the agouti colors we see today are certainly anything but mud-colored.

Domestic Cavies

There are three basic kinds of domestic Cavies, grouped according to hair type and length.

1. The American, English or Bolivian Cavy

The popularity of this Cavy can be demonstrated by the fact that no less than three countries have named him as their own. The known and most widely raised strain, he is characterized by a short-haired, smooth coat. There are twenty recognized color varieties. The most common is the white (or albino), which is used in research laboratories and hospitals and which commercial breeders raise almost exclusively. Some of the other more popular and widely distributed colors are black, red, fawn, cream, gray, brindle brown, silver agouti and golden agouti.

2. The Abyssinian Cavy

The Abby is distinguished from other varieties by its harsh, wiry coat, not unlike that of a wire terrier. The rough hair swirls like little cowlicks into well-formed rosettes, each one radiating from a distinct and tiny center. Stiff erect hairs make up the ruff or collar (across the shoulders) and the back ridge (across the hindquarters). The hair from the back of the head to the collar or ruff is called the mane; between collar and back ridge is the ridge. (The divisions are created by the outer edges of the rosettes.) There isn't any "right" number of rosettes to watch for—in fact, the more rosettes the better, as long as they are single and distinct.

3. The Peruvian Cavy

Considered by many to be the most beautiful of all the varieties of Cavies, its coat is straight, long and silky, measuring up to 36 inches over the hindquarters. The coat should part from the spine and flow down the sides like a mane; it should be of such a length that at a glance it is difficult to know which end of the animal you're looking at!

This type of Cavy is kept only by the most sincere fancier, because of the considerable amount of time that must be devoted to its care. To remain at its best, the fine silky long hair should be brushed daily and washed and set at least once a month. In addition, the Peruvian is rather delicate, and must be guarded against drafts and dampness more diligently than his hardier cousins.

The most popular Peruvian colors are black, red, white, orange, cream and slate, but the length of the coat, rather than the color, is the more important factor contributing to the Peruvian's beauty—in fact, the Peruvian is commonly called the "Silky."

English Cavy—Tri-color.   Peruvian Cavy—Orange.

Color types

1. Agouti

This type is named after a South American rodent with grizzled hair, and is considered to belong to the same type as the original animals found in South America by the Spanish. There are three recognized agouti colors: Golden, Silver and Cinnamon. In each, the tip and base of each individual hair is black, with a bar of color in the middle—this gives the coat its ticked effect. In each case, too, the belly of the Cavy is its basic color—rich golden, pale silver, or cinnamon (reddish-brown).

2. Self

"Self" is the term applied to the solid-color coat of these Cavies, the most popular and most widely bred. There are two reasons for their popularity: first, it is not as difficult to produce the solid colors as it is to produce patterns or unusual markings, and second, in breeding, the Self's shade, size, shape and coat can be more easily controlled than other breeds'. At present, there are seven Self colors: black, white, chocolate, red, beige, cream and lilac. Through many years of careful breeding, the colors have been well established, and are perfectly pure, bright and rich.

Hair markings

1. Dutch

The Dutch Cavy's name is derived from its markings, which are similar to those of the Dutch Rabbit. Dutch Cavies have been bred in five recognized colors: black, red, chocolate, silver agouti and red and black agouti. The cheeks, ears and hindquarters are the basic color, with an underlying background which forms a band or saddle around the middle and a strip down the front of the face.

This particular variety is rather difficult to breed absolutely true to pattern, and the demand far exceeds the supply. The distinctive markings of the Dutch Cavy make it very beautiful and a true challenge to the breeder.

2. Himalayan

Like the Dutch Cavy, the Himalayan Cavy also derives its name from a rabbit with similar markings. The markings are color patches on the nose, feet and ears. These vary from a pale buff to a very dark brown or black. The rest of the coat is pure white. The Himalayan breeds true to type; fortunately for Cavy lovers, Himalayans are in good supply.

The need to belong: this Cavy prefers to crowd into the bowl with the others rather than stay by himself.

3. Tortoise-and-White

This breed, one of the oldest and most popular, is easy to raise, but it presents a challenge to the breeder because it is difficult to reproduce an even pattern.

A good Tortoise-and-White should have between six and ten black, red and white square-cut patches; these should be of equal size and run alternately down each side.

Because of the difficulty in breeding the Tortoise-and-White, a perfectly marked specimen can be worth quite a bit of money. But whether or not you have a grand champion, you'll find this Cavy one of the most fascinating and most beautiful of all.

2 The Cavy in research

Just as we've become accustomed to the name Cavy, we'll have to reverse face for a moment and call him a guinea pig—in the laboratory sense of the word, that is. Tame, easy to breed and easy to control as he is, the Cavy has long been used as a research tool by scientists. In fact, to insure a constant supply of Cavies, many of the larger hospitals and labs—including those of the Army— have had to establish their own breeding colonies.

The original "guinea pig"

The Cavy has served as guinea pig in many fields of study, includ- ing cosmetics, drugs, hormone treatment, allergy and immuni- zation, but his greatest contribution has been in the field of nutritional research. Because he is unable to synthesize ascorbic acid (Vitamin C), he has been an ideal subject for the study of C deficiency (scurvy). He also has unusually high requirements for certain amino acids, minerals and vitamins (arginine, folic acid, potassium, thiamine and a substance called the "grass juice factor"). Finally, the Cavy's development at birth is extremely advanced for a mammal, so that many experiments can be carried out almost from the time he is born.

The white (albino) American Self Cavy is the type most widely used in the laboratory. Skin reactions and tattoo identification numbers are easily seen on white skin, and mongrel genetic lines and inbred (pure) strains are most easily distinguished in the white Cavy. Pure lines are usually preferred for research experiments, because there is a higher probability of uniform response when the animals used are as much alike as possible.

For the future

The Cavy's future as a research animal has been the subject of some debate. The demand for smaller rodents such as the rat, mouse, hamster and gerbil has been great during recent years, and both the mouse and the rat hold leads over the Cavy as laboratory favorites. There are several reasons for this: for one thing, researchers have often had to use smaller rodents in order to utilize their space most efficiently. Another factor often considered is the ability of the smaller rodents to breed far more rapidly than the Cavy. Finally, scientists have been forced to turn to other animals because of the scarcity of quality Cavies; stock raised in commercial colonies has not always met the exacting standards of research laboratories.

Perhaps this will change in the near future as more commercial breeders improve their facilities. Today, the breeding records and feeding and weaning schedules of many commercial colonies are being computerized, and housing facilities have also been greatly improved. Animals intended for breeding are delivered by Caesarian section and raised by hand. The breeders are then housed in either stainless steel or fiberglass pens in completely controlled and monitored environments. With the initiation of such improvements, we can be sure that the Cavy will continue to play a major role in the world of health research.

3 Housing

Although the Cavy's South American range extends from the tropical to the semi-tropical, his hardiness has enabled him to thrive in more temperate zones as well, because climate and altitude are not nearly as important to the health of your Cavy as

This type of cage is frequently used in the laboratory. It can house either a pair or a sow and her litter.

is proper care. Of course, he does have certain housing and environmental requirements, and these should be considered well in advance, so that you will have his pen and living area ready before making your final visit to the pet store.

The environment

Only in the warmer climates—tropical and semi-tropical—can the Cavy be successfully kept outdoors unprotected all year round. Anywhere else, some type of housing must be provided, and certain general rules should be followed to insure the animals' comfort.

The first three rules of thumb are easy to remember:
1. Keep the area clean and sanitary.
2. Keep the area dry and free from drafts.
3. Keep the temperature between 60° and 85°F; the ideal temperature is 68° to 72°F. If the temperature goes above 90°F, heat prostration will probably result; pregnant sows

are particularly susceptible. At temperatures below 55°F, youngsters grow poorly, litter size usually falls, and the reproduction rate itself decreases.

Even more important than the actual temperature is that it remain constant, for Cavies are very sensitive to change. Increased moisture, temperature fluctuations and drafts must be avoided; Cavies kept under such conditions will be very susceptible to colds and other illnesses.

The fourth Golden Rule for housing is to limit the number of animals per pen: six to eight females and one male to a pen is the limit. There should never be more than one male at a time in a pen, because when two males are together they will fight. If a male is kept with a number of females, the females should be moved as soon as they show signs of pregnancy, in order to avoid the danger of premature births. After the young have been weaned, the mother can be returned to the pen with the male.

Let there be light

If it is not possible to house your Cavies in such a way that they

Don't leave your pet Cavy unguarded outdoors.

will receive indirect sunlight, try to provide them with an adequate substitute. Two satisfactory artificial lighting set-ups are the following:

1. A fluorescent lamp with two 40-watt bulbs, set up 3 feet above the floor of the cage.
2. A fluorescent lamp with two 40-watt daylight bulbs on each side; and two 6-watt incandescent daylight bulbs 6 inches from either side of the fluorescent fixture. (All bulbs should be 3 feet above the floor of the cage.)

If this type of direct overhead lighting is not practical for the kind of housing you have selected, indirect lighting from the side of the cage will have to do. In each 24-hour period, provide 14 hours of light and 10 hours of darkness. This cycle has been found best for breeding.

The pollution problem

We're all beset with noise and air pollution headaches these days, and pets—especially city animals—are our fellow victims. Try at all times to protect your Cavies from loud or sudden noises. If you live in an area where the pollution level is high, provide the same protection for your Cavies as you do for yourself. Optimal conditions would include filtered, thermostatically regulated fresh air circulating freely through the cages and conditioning the environment. Unfortunately, such perfect conditions can seldom be maintained, and your Cavy will simply make his peace with pollution as best he can—just as you do.

Caging

There are basically two ways to house your Cavies: in hutches or pens. Because Cavies do not climb, jump or gnaw on wood, their homes do not need to be elaborate, as long as they are cozy and provide the pets with room in which to spread out.

Minimum desirable housing requirements

4 sows and 1 boar	1.7 sq ft per animal
Single adult (800 gr)	1.0 sq ft per animal
Litterbearing female	2.5 to 3.0 sq ft

| 200 gr weanling | 0.3 sq ft |
| 400 gr weanling | 0.5 sq ft |

Since Cavies spend much of their time running around, a great deal of floor space should be provided. This space can be expanded by building ramps or stairways to connect the floor with an upper level or shelf, about 4 inches from the floor, preferably in a dark corner. It serves a dual purpose: Cavies like to use it as a perch (in much the same way as birds do), and it provides a kind of play area above, while the lower level is used for nesting and feeding.

Hutches

These are completely closed units. An indoor hutch may be constructed of wire mesh with wooden door frames and posts; an outdoor summer hutch may be all weatherproof wood with a wire mesh door.

If you decide to build a hutch, allow at least 15 inches from the floor to the ceiling to insure proper ventilation. A hutch 4 feet long by 2 feet wide by 15 inches high will provide ample space for four sows and one boar. To save space, you can easily build a tier of up to four hutches; just be sure to allow at least 4 inches below and above each hutch for proper ventilation.

Pens

Pens, like hutches, come in many sizes and shapes, but all have open tops for easy feeding and cleaning (and since Cavies don't climb or jump, you don't have to worry about their escaping). The floor of a single pen should be at least 2 feet off the ground: this will save you a lot of bending while you are cleaning, feeding or observing, and the height will also help prevent floor drafts.

In most commercial breeding colonies tiered pens are used, because many more Cavies can be kept and bred per unit of floor space. The pens are either directly over one another or stepped back; in either case, there should be at least 4 inches between pens. Tier pens can be constructed of wood, but fiberglass or stainless steel are easier to clean and sterilize.

If you expect to raise Cavies in large numbers, plan to visit several breeders who have had various kinds of pens in operation

Two are twice as much fun as one, and they don't take up much more room.

for some time so that you can see which type is most applicable to your particular situation.

Cages

Many kinds of metal cages are commercially available. Some types have wire floors. These are undesirable and should be removed, but the removable metal trays below make for easy cleaning. In general, Cavies are best kept on solid floors to help protect them from drafts.

New on the market are small all-plastic cages with metal tops. This type of cage is somewhat expensive, but is excellent for single Cavies or for one pair. It can also serve as a "delivery cage" for a single pregnant female. The construction of this cage insures freedom from drafts, and clean food and water can be supplied at all times.

One of the cheapest and most easily obtained "cages" (especially for apartment dwellers) is a glass aquarium with or without a removable lid. A long 20-gallon tank (30″ × 12″ × 12″) is just the right size for a pair of adults.

Housekeeping

Remember, whether you build your Cavy's home from discarded packing crates or buy the most expensive stainless steel pens, the key to a well-run pen is cleanliness. Your Cavies are captive, and must depend on you to clean their cage regularly—at least once a week—and provide the proper bedding materials. As they produce relatively large amounts of urine, neglect on your part can make life extremely miserable for them and odorous for you.

While you are cleaning the cage, the Cavies can be housed in other cages or placed in a clean cardboard box. Periodically, after cleaning the pen, apply an agreeable non-odor-producing disin-

Cavies readily learn to use a suck bottle.

fectant. To insure your pet's safety, use one produced for cat use, such as the kind sold to deodorize kitty litter pans; these are available in pet departments.

Bedding materials

Shavings. This material is favored for young Cavies and non-pregnant females. (Some breeders have reported irritation to females about to deliver.) Coarse white pine shavings are recommended by the National Research Council Institute of Laboratory Animal Resources. Other acceptable kinds are cedar, basswood and poplar shavings.

Sawdust. This is undesirable. Because of its tendency to mat when wet, it must be changed often.

Hay or straw. If either of these is used, it must be changed twice a week, or as soon as it begins to get wet.

Chaff. This is one of the smoothest and least irritating types of bedding, but is usually not easy to find. It also absorbs better than most materials. Droppings and urine will sink to the bottom, leaving the surface dry.

Peanut shells. These are excellent and economical (if you like peanuts!). They are absorbent, do not mat, and last longer than any other material.

Cat litter. The material sold for use in cat pans is a type of treated fullers' earth. It is rather hard, but as it is very absorbent, it makes an excellent base. Cover a layer of this with hay or straw and you'll have excellent results.

Other good bedding materials are peat moss, dried shredded sugar-cane, and crushed corn cobs.

Now that you've provided clean and comfortable quarters for your Cavies, check to make sure that no rodents, dogs or cats can get near the cage. A Cavy is a defenseless beastie, and if attacked can only try to hide. But if the cage is critter- and draft-proof, you're ready to bring your friends to their new home.

4 Food for thought

The Cavy is one of the easiest pets to keep in the house as far as feeding is concerned. There's no guesswork about his diet—thanks to his years of work as a laboratory research animal, his nutritional requirements have been established exactly. Although your pet can survive on a diet of ordinary lawn clippings, only a variety of the right foods will keep him healthy. A good balanced diet will consist of a commercially prepared pellet or chow, supplemented by fresh greens, water and salt.

The Cavy's nutritional requirements are listed in the following chart:

Protein	20 to 25% of the diet
Fat	3 to 5% of the diet
Carbohydrates	28 to 55% of the diet
Minerals and ash	7 to 9% of the diet
Vitamin A	2 mg/kg body weight daily
Vitamin E	2 mg daily
Vitamin C	1 mg/100 gr body weight, up to 25 mg daily
Vitamin K	50 mg/kg ration
Choline	0.10 to 0.15 gr/100 gr ration
Folic acid	0.3 to 0.6 mg/100 gr ration
Niacin	2 mg/100 gr ration
Pantothenic acid	1 to 2 mg/100 gr ration
Pyridoine	1.6 mg/100 gr ration
Riboflavin	0.3 mg/100 gr ration
Thiamine	200 mg/100 gr ration

No matter what anyone may tell you, it's simply not possible to make a cheap home mixture that is equal in nutritional value to commercial feeds. Some Cavy owners have fed their pets solely on oats, hay and water, but I feel this is a serious mistake—imagine what a diet of bread and water would do to your own health! Obviously, the most sensible thing you can do is purchase pellets or chow specifically made for Cavies (*not* for mice, hamsters or rabbits), since only these formulas are designed to meet the requirements listed above. When you purchase food, always check the label to see if all requirements have been met. If not, look for another brand.

Carrots are considered "green" food, and they are very good for your pet.

What about rabbit pellets?

Many Cavy owners have heard that whatever is good for rabbits is good for Cavies. Let's consider this for a moment. Although rabbit pellets and Cavy pellets are generally similar, there are two important differences. First of all, there is no Vitamin C added to the formula in rabbit pellets, and—this can never be emphasized too strongly—while rabbits can manufacture Vitamin C in their bodies, Cavies, like man, must have Vitamin C added to the diet in order to live. The other difference is that the fiber content of rabbit pellets is much higher. For these two reasons, rabbit pellets should not be fed for long periods of time. They may be used as a temporary diet if you are sure that you can supply Vitamin C in another form (by feeding kale, cabbage or orange peel each day, for example—at least 1 ounce per Cavy).

Green food

If you want to see your pets flourish, be sure that they get green food at least once a day. According to many Cavy experts, the

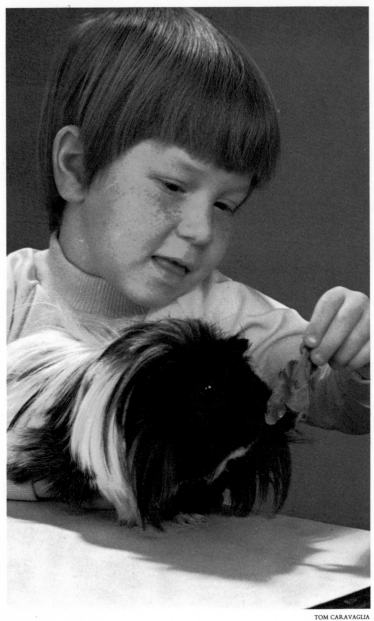

Not all Cavies like cabbage.

best green foods are kale and cabbage. (These two foods combined have been shown to prevent hair loss in nursing females.) To be sure, cabbage has caused some discussion. The anti-cabbage party argues that it spoils very easily and is generally not a good food for Cavies. Here, the best policy is one you'll want to follow with any new food: feed a small quantity to your pet, and see whether he likes it. If he categorically rejects it time after time, simply don't give him any more.

Your pet's diet doesn't have to be boring. To find out what he likes and what is good for him, experiment with different types of fresh foods (except for potatoes, onions and peppers. He won't like those). Lettuce, that old reliable among the green foods, does supply bulk and water, but actually contains very few nutrients, and should only be fed as a treat along with a complete dry diet and other fresh greens.

"Green" foods aren't all colored green, by the way. The list encompasses many others, including roots such as carrots, beets and turnips. Explore your area to find out what green foods are available; some of the more commonly used are green alfalfa, cabbage, kale, celery tops, cauliflower, green corn stalks and leaves, lawn clippings, plantain, clover, dandelion, sprouted oats, spinach, broccoli, tomatoes, parsley and apples. Ask yourself in each case, "Would I eat this? Is it clean and free of pesticides?" If you can answer yes, go ahead and ring the dinner bell, but start with small portions, and remember whether you liked spinach, Brussels sprouts and asparagus the first time you tried them.

Feed supplements

If you can't get green foods in the winter, perhaps you can locate a feed store or farmer who will sell you meadow hay, timothy hay, dry corn, bran or barley meal. These are all good feed supplements with or without greens. Timothy hay is the most important, since the seeds and leaves can be used first as feed and the stems can then be used for bedding.

If you run out of packaged food, your Cavy can easily get along with an assortment of green foods and dry supplements such as stale bread until you are able to stock in his chow again. Try to keep such emergency periods down to no more than two days, though.

Feeding methods

You can set out your pet's dry food in closed food hoppers or in open bowls. If you do decide to use open bowls, however, provide heavy ceramic bowls or dog dishes, as plastic bowls can be tipped over or chewed up. And be alert: Cavies tend to sit in open bowls and soil their dinners! You should make a little holder for the hay, rather than leave it on the floor of the cage where it can be soiled.

Water

The question of "free water" is a controversial one: some owners feel that their Cavies get enough water from the vegetables and fruits provided. My experience is that they can, but I feel that even so they should not be maintained without water. The problem, simply, is this: Cavies can only consume a certain volume of material in a 24-hour day. If you stuff them with green food, they will have very little room left for the two ounces of dry food that each one requires; and when less than two ounces of dry food is consumed per day, nutritional disorders (reduced litter size, hair loss and slow growth) will result—a nightmare for the commercial breeder and the pet owner alike. What's the surest means of prevention? Simply supply free water. The Cavy will take it if he needs it.

The water requirement for an adult Cavy is about four–six ounces daily. The best way to supply this water, whether you have one Cavy or one thousand Cavies, is through a glass bottle and stainless steel tube with an adjustable tip. (The Cavy must lick the tip to get the water.) Tubes with free flow, known as "suck bottles," are often sold in pet stores; they are inexpensive, particularly those with plastic tips. But it is best not to use these. If no stainless steel is available, use glass. The best tubes I know feature a ball bearing in the tip which the Cavy licks. It prevents the back flow of debris from the Cavy's mouth, so that very little bacterial growth collects in the bottle. This is not only the best arrangement for your thirsty friends, but will also save you some extra work, for the bottle will only need washing once a week rather than every day. Do change the water every day, though.

Finally, try to keep a salt spool (such as those sold for rabbits) available for each group of Cavies. If they need it, they'll use it.

The Big Four of feeding: (quantity)

1. Dry commercial food ("guinea pig pellets"), daily — 2 oz
2. Green food, daily — 2–3 oz
3. Water in bottles with stainless steel or glass tube, daily — $\frac{1}{2}$ pint
4. Hay, other dry food supplements — free feeding, as available

Cavies are curious about everything that goes on.

5   Choosing your Cavy

Once you've built or bought that perfect cage and stocked up the pantry, you still need to find the perfect tenant. The choice won't be easy: you may find yourself standing in a pet store or commercial breeder's building, looking at several Cavies—and liking them all. Which one is for you?

Your first Cavy

A good argument can be made for every type, but if you're a novice in the field of Cavy raising, you'll probably do best to start with the short-haired American Self Cavy. The short-hair coat and Self colors are easy to breed and care for. If you are thinking of breeding on a large scale, remember that the Self White is widely used in research, and extra youngsters can be sold easily. As you gain experience, though, you may want to try other colors or combinations.

Once you've had some success in breeding and raising Americans, you'll be ready for the Abyssinian. The Ab or Abby represents a greater challenge for the breeder, and his coat may take a bit more caring for (though not much).

Finally, the true fancier of beauty will ultimately want to try his hand with the queen of all Cavies, the Peruvian. A word of caution: before you take on a Peruvian, remember that its hair must be put up in curlers after three months of age and taken down daily for brushing. If you have the time and patience to devote to a Peruvian, you'll undoubtedly reap a great deal of pleasure from your hobby.

Which sex to choose?

Even if you're a beginner, you'll probably want two Cavies—one male, one female—so that you can breed them. To observe the behavior of the mother during pregnancy, delivery and nursing and to watch the Cavies rearing their young is an unforgettable experience for the pet-owning family. If circumstances make it impossible for you to bring home more than one Cavy, however, don't despair: bachelor Cavies can get along handsomely if given enough human attention and affection. If you're not planning to raise a brood, it doesn't matter whether you choose a male or a female Cavy—they're equally lovable and responsive.

Cavy shows

Unfortunately, city dwellers don't have much opportunity to attend Cavy shows. These are usually rural functions, often held in conjunction with poultry displays at county fairs. If you should have the opportunity to attend one, by all means go. It will be well worth your while. You will see more of a variety of color and coat types than you imagined existed. And best of all, you will have an opportunity to talk to the breeders, people who love their animals and enjoy talking about them.

Acquiring basic breeding stock, or even a pet, at one of these shows, will give you an opportunity to see the strain from which your own particular pet has been bred. You can be quite sure that only the finest Cavies are brought to the show, and if you buy stock there, it is almost certain you will be getting healthy animals.

Pet shops

If you can not attend a show or visit a breeding establishment (known as a caviary), you can still find good stock at your local pet shop or pet department. Most of the animals sold through pet departments are quite young, six to twelve weeks old, and selected for attractiveness and condition. Of course, you must use your own judgment to a certain extent. Be sure that the shop you deal with is clean and well-lighted, and that the cage from which you pick your pet is in good condition. The animals should be alert, energetic, aware of your approach, and should whistle vigorously when you try to pick them up. Avoid cages where the Cavies are listless, huddled together, have bald spots, sores, mucousy noses, raspy breath, constant panting. When picked up, a healthy Cavy should feel solid and meaty, except possibly for very young specimens less than two weeks old. These latter, by the way, are always chancy. Even though a Cavy can eat almost as soon as it is whelped, it still should be with its mother for a week or two to get a good start. If the Cavy's skin is loose on the bones, if you can feel the ribs, if it feels limp in your hand or has a big pot belly, avoid this animal. In fact, if there are too many like that in the enclosure, best look elsewhere.

Check for disposition

When selecting for temperament, take a few minutes to study the herd. Moving slowly and smoothly—avoid any jerky or sudden movements—extend your hand toward a particular Cavy. If it is interested and alert and, while aware of your hand, somewhat suspicious of it (for after all, Cavies are shy), chances are it will tame easily. However, a Cavy that responds to a proferred hand by dashing madly about the cage may be too nervous and high-strung, and though it may be fine for breeding, it would probably not be as satisfactory a pet as a calmer one. Disposition does run in strains, Cavies from certain strains being noticeably calmer and gentler than those of other strains. Of course, even the calmest and best-natured Cavy can be ruined by improper handling and teasing, while even a nervous, high-strung animal will improve, with gentle handling.

The healthy candidate

Always check the teeth before you buy a Cavy. As is the case with all rodents, his teeth grow continually to replace the portion worn away by chewing. Sometimes, for one reason or another, the teeth are not worn down properly or do not meet properly. This can result in overgrown teeth, a potential source of trouble. Also, occasionally a tooth will be broken, and there is a good chance that it may not grow back properly. Avoid Cavies with tooth troubles.

An animal that constantly holds its head to one side or shakes its head may have problems—pass it by. A good Cavy has bright button eyes. When he doesn't feel well, they may be dull, teary or mucousy. Make sure the eyes are wide open and that the area around the eyes isn't wet or slimy.

The Cavy's legs are short and set well under him; when he runs they are almost impossible to see. But you can judge by the backline. This should remain level as he moves; if it bobs up and down, there is something wrong with his legs. It may not be serious, but

Handle your prospective purchase for a few minutes before you make a final selection.

you'd do well not to take a chance. Look for the Cavy that runs swiftly and smoothly.

Get them young

Finally, try to get your pets young—before they are twelve weeks

A good Cavy has bright button eyes and a sleek shiny coat, and looks lively and alert.

old. This way you'll be able to breed them at the proper time. Also, your well-balanced feeding program will yield the best results if you have young animals, since older ones may have been poorly fed before coming to you or may be accustomed to another diet and therefore fare badly with yours. You'll gain a lot of knowledge just watching your Cavy mature, and with the next Cavy (or herd) you'll be able to apply all that you've learned with the first pet. In a word: start small, and grow with your investment.

6 Handling and grooming

Until your Cavy gets to know you, he will be shy, as many animals are, and will probably try to hide or retreat to a corner of his cage at the sound of strange feet approaching. Be patient and give him a chance to get acquainted. With kindness and care, you will win his trust and friendship.

Getting to know you

When you first bring your pet home, make sure he has fresh food, water and bedding. Don't leave him alone. Allow him a quiet day or two to get used to his new surroundings without picking him up, but do pay him an introductory call as soon as possible. Approach the cage slowly, talking softly and reassuringly to him. Any sudden or boisterous movements may throw him into a panic, and if there are any young around, they may be trampled in the rush. Reach into the cage and give him a hand to sniff. Now slowly place your hand over his shoulders; gently close your hand and lift the Cavy firmly, placing your other hand under his body for support. If lifted in this manner, your pet will feel secure and rest quietly.

An alternate, and by some a preferred method, is to cradle the Cavy upside down, like a baby, in the crook of your arm (see illustration). With his feet up in the air, he won't struggle. He'll enjoy being held and stroked—but don't squeeze him, or he'll try to wriggle out of the embrace.

Finally, be sure to protect him from falling at all times. Cavies have no way to shield themselves from the impact of a fall, and of course they can not land on their feet the way cats can, so a fall will almost certainly end in painful bruises and even broken bones. If, in spite of all precautions, your pet does meet with a crash landing and appears to be in pain, check with your veterinarian. In the event of a bruise, the best prescription is soft, clean bedding, good food and plenty of rest.

Training

As lovable as the Cavy is, he is not as quick to catch on to lessons as some of his rodent relatives. Still, one European fancier declares that anyone who thinks Cavies are dull-witted obviously hasn't spent any time with them. This much is sure, in any event: with patient guidance, your little friend will learn a trick or two to delight you. Many owners have taught their Cavies to squeak when green food is offered; you may even be able to show off a pet who sits up and whistles whenever you open the refrigerator or wrinkle a plastic bag.

The best training method is one which has been developed in scientific experiments with animals. We discuss it here in detail on page 56 under the heading *Operant conditioning*.

To bathe or not to bathe?

Many pet owners, bath-conscious as they are, tend to think animals need a frequent tubbing as well. Actually, Cavies are among the cleanest of animals, and the only time yours may really need a bath is when you have not changed the bedding or cleaned the cage regularly, and the Cavy's hair becomes soiled. In that case use warm water and a good mild soap on the dirt. To be sure that you do not get water in his ears, put a little plug of cotton in them. Rinse with warm water until all traces of soap are removed from the fur. Then rub the Cavy as dry as possible with a clean

Most Cavies seem quite relaxed when held this way, and make no attempt to struggle.

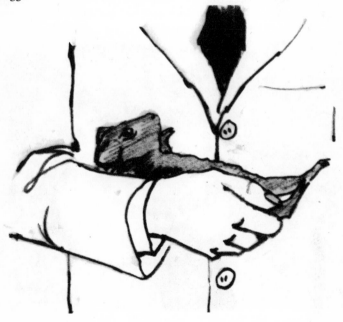

towel. Finally, let him rest in a warm place (75 to 80°F.)—one that is free from any air currents—until he is completely dry. An old shoe box lined with a dry towel makes a good spot.

The well-kept coat

Half a teaspoon of linseed or cod-liver oil in the Cavy's diet daily will add greatly to the luster and body of his coat. Another simple way to help your pet keep his coat smooth and shining is to rub the animal from his nose down his back with the palm of your hand. Not only will this do wonders for his fur, but he will become more tame and affectionate as he becomes accustomed to being handled.

American and Abyssinian Cavies will get along famously with simple grooming measures and—if necessary—a very occasional cleaning bath; you may want to run a toothbrush through the Abby's rosettes from time to time. The Peruvian, on the other hand, needs a daily brushing as well as a shampoo and set at least once a month. Use a baby or tearless shampoo. Afterwards, its

Cavies are usually very peaceful, but occasionally two old boars will struggle for dominance. When this happens, they must be separated or they will inflict nasty wounds on one another.

TOM CARAVAGLIA

How not to handle your Cavy! Held like this, he could fall and injure himself.

Polydactylism, or the growth of an extra toe, is a recessive trait that can appear as a result of inbreeding.

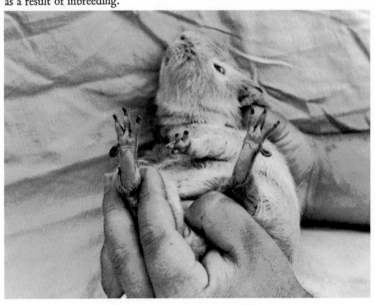

hair must be brushed and untangled; use a soft baby brush, never a wire brush or comb. "Curlers" can be made out of small rolls of paper, or you can tie the Cavy's hair up in rags. Brushing will help any breed of Cavy, but it is absolutely essential to maintain a healthy Peruvian.

A home away from home

If you must transport your Cavy—to a show, for example— you'll want to make the excursion as painless as possible. A travel case such as those sold for cats (or you can build your own) will easily accomodate him; a Cavy can travel comfortably for up to two days in a cage with 0.5 square feet of floor space, as long as proper ventilation and good food are supplied. He can travel several days without water as well, if you provide some juicy carrots or apples for moisture.

If you plan extensive traveling or camping, it would be advisable to leave the pets at home and ask a good friend or responsible neighbor to give them fresh bedding, food and water at regular intervals. If you plan to move to a distant city or town, you can arrange to have your Cavies shipped by air express.

7 Health and first aid

Cavies are remarkably healthy critters, and any troubles that arise can usually be traced to improper feeding or care. The best guard against illness—for Cavies as for human beings—is that proverbial ounce of prevention. Provide it diligently and you will probably never have to refer to this chapter for any reason other than idle curiosity.

Symptoms

If an animal becomes droopy, has a rough coat, eats little or nothing, appears bloated or, conversely, emaciated, or has soft droppings, he should be suspect. (Normally a Cavy's droppings are dry and virtually odorless.)

Nutritional deficiencies

Barbering. This may occur when Cavies kept on wire floors are deprived of hay or other roughage. The young may be completely stripped of hair by the adults. Under these conditions, adults will also strip one another.

Hair loss. If hair is lost over the entire body, this is probably due to vitamin deficiencies. Make sure your pet is getting an adequate diet.

Scurvy. This Vitamin C deficiency usually occurs during the winter months, when greens rich in Vitamin C are hard to find. For this reason, some breeders suggest adding a crushed Vitamin C tablet (250 mg) to the animals' drinking water each day.

Overgrowth of teeth. This results from a lack of chewing matter in the diet. If the diet is not corrected (by supplying hay or other roughage), the front teeth can grow to the point where the Cavy can no longer close his mouth and will literally die of starvation.

Diarrhea. This can usually be traced to too many greens in the animal's diet, though it can also be the result of a cold. Cut out leafy greens. Administer castor oil, ½ tsp. for adults and 12–20 drops for young (depending on size and age), and put the animal on clean dry bedding.

Constipation. This is very rare. If it occurs, feed the Cavy a little apple peel or olive oil to get things started again.

Colds and pneumonia. These are usually caused by changes in temperature, humidity or ventilation. If your Cavy has a dry, husky cough, bed him on meadow hay and keep the temperature constant, with a boiling kettle or vaporizer nearby, so the air does not become too dry.

Tuberculosis. May develop from pneumonia. If an animal does not recover from pneumonia, but remains emaciated and ill, it will probably be best to put him to sleep, particularly if his presence endangers the entire colony.

Coccidiosis (*Eimeria cavidae*). This protozoan disease is spread through contaminated foods. Affected animals develop a watery diarrhea, become listless, and lose their appetite. The disease is spread through spores shed in the droppings. When the Cavy licks his feet, as all rodents do, he becomes infected or reinfected. Absolute cleanliness is therefore essential. Change the bedding as soon as it becomes soiled, or better yet, when you do suspect

Overleaf: A heart-to-heart conversation.

coccidiosis, keep the colony on wire screening; scrub the screening regularly to eliminate spores. Eventually resistance will be built up. And, of course, consult your vet.

Salmonellosis. This bacterial infection is probably the most common lethal disease among Cavies, and will often destroy entire colonies. Symptoms include weakness, diarrhea and temperature rise. See your vet.

Parasites:

Scabies. This is caused by a microscopic mite. If your pet has scabby sores and scratches or appears itchy, try dipping him in a rotenone solution as for lice, or dust him regularly with rotenone powder.

Lice. They are usually hard to locate. Inspect your Cavies regularly, especially around the ears, eyes and lower abdomen, for long, thin moving objects. The eggs (nits) may be seen as translucent globules on dark hair. Control is difficult but possible: dip the animals in a water mixture of 2 ounces of 3 to 5% rotenone per gallon of water. A single dipping will usually do. At the same time, clean the pens and dust them with rotenone, or use a cat dip or spray.

Fleas and ticks. If these show up, they are being carried in from the outside. Any insecticidal spray or powder packaged for cats is suitable for Cavies, but do not use dog products. While cats and Cavies lick themselves, dogs do not, so more toxic materials may be used on dogs.

Wounds. These are seldom a problem, but can sometimes occur as the result of fighting. Cut away the surrounding hair, cleanse the wound thoroughly with green soap and apply a mild antiseptic as you would to a cut on your finger.

Bruises. Give the Cavy plenty of rest and good food, so that his body can do a proper job of healing.

Falls. If any bones seem broken, consult your vet.

Poisons. Consult the veterinarian immediately. Try to be able to tell him which poison is involved.

Many of the symptoms for various ailments are similar, and even those who are trained sometimes have difficulty in diagnosing. Call on your veterinarian in your time of need: he can recommend the measures needed to control and eliminate the disorder. In the case of some diseases, the best procedure may be to dispose of the infected animals quickly and humanely. But again, if you follow the guidelines for disease prevention, you will probably never have any problem more serious than a brief sniffle.

Rules to remember for disease prevention:

1. Start your colony with healthy stock.
2. Keep pens and food containers clean.
3. Keep other pets and rodents away.
4. Provide adequate space.
5. Do not overbreed.
6. Provide fresh drinking water daily.
7. Feed a balanced diet of dry and green foods.

8 Breeding Cavies

Many people believe that Cavies are as prolific as the legendary rabbit, but it just ain't so. In fact, in comparison to other rodents, Cavies' families are few and far between. The hamster can bear a litter of 1 to 12 young every 15 to 18 days; the mouse and rat come close behind, followed by the rabbit (with possibly 1 to 13 young every 30 to 35 days); but the Cavy needs about 68 days and bears litters of 1 to 9 weanlings, with an average of only 3.

The estrus cycle

All female mammals go through a period called the estrus (heat) cycle. Some mammals have only one such cycle each year while others, such as the Cavy, are polyestrous—they have cycles all year round. In the Cavy, the estrus cycle starts at about 68 days of age, and repeats every 16 to 19 days. At one point during the cycle (the first 6 to 15 hours for the Cavy), estrus occurs; at that time, the female becomes very restless and prowls about the cage. If her back is stroked she will lower it so that her spine appears concave. At this time she is receptive to the male. Ovulation, or egg release, must accompany estrus, or no young can result.

An example of inherited congenital blindness. Inbreeding in itself is not harmful, but it does increase the chance that a defective recessive gene carried by both parents will be expressed in the young.

Although Cavy babies can eat solid food within two or three days of birth, they really should nurse for at least 20, and even up to 30, days.

The male attains sexual maturity by about two months of age. During mating, he deposits sperm in the female, and these fertilize (unite with) the eggs she releases. The estrus cycle will be interrupted at this point for a 65- to 70-day gestation (development) period, during which time the embryo develops from a single cell to a complete individual. Within six to eight hours following the birth of the litter, the female has estrus again. If she is bred at this time, she can become pregnant again immediately.

When to breed?

There are no real problems for the novice in breeding Cavies except possibly the question of *when* to breed. If you are in no great rush to hear the patter of tiny paws, wait at least 12 weeks before breeding a female. It is best to separate the sexes during this time so that they can grow and develop without fighting.

One pointer will help you get started: breed your females before they reach full maturity at five months. If they are bred at three months, they will have their first litters before maturity and the birth will be easier as the pelvis will not yet have fused.

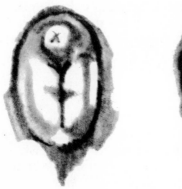

Sexing Cavies. Male left, female right.

Sexing your Cavies

In the beginning you may have some trouble distinguishing

between males and females. To sex a Cavy, take the animal in your left hand and turn it on its back, resting the head against your body. Both male and female have a genital slit shaped like an inverted "Y." Press gently in front of this slit: if the Cavy is male, the penis will then protrude between the two branches of the "Y." (Never try to sex the young in this manner before they are three weeks old.)

Breeding Methods

Monogamous pairs. One female and one male are placed together. This is an excellent method for the novice with only a few Cavies. The fancier who is trying to develop a specific color or hair type will also use this method to insure a close control of genetics. The commercial breeder, on the other hand, only uses this type of breeding for foundation animals in establishing new colonies.

Polygamous groups. A number of sows are mated to one boar. These colonies are established with twelve-week-old animals who will remain together for their entire reproductive life. The best combination seems to be three sows and one boar, but groups of up to forty sows and one boar have been successful. The most important factor for polygamous breeding is the amount of floor space provided: it should never be less than 1.7 square feet per sow. Also, remember that the larger the group, the more difficulty you'll have in controlling infectious disease.

The first litter

You'll have no trouble telling when a female has become pregnant—she'll begin to bulge almost immediately. At this point, keep a particularly close eye on her diet to make sure she receives all the nutritional elements she needs. (Stale bread soaked in milk is a desirable dry food supplement.) Although the father and mother can be left together through pregnancy and throughout the birth process, many Cavy owners recommend providing a separate cage for the mother several weeks before delivery. If you would like to breed her again immediately following the birth of the litter, this must be done within the first eight hours after delivery. If post-partum mating is allowed, a Cavy can produce as many as five litters a year, otherwise the average is about three and a half.

The Cavy seems to be quite secretive about the birth of its young, by the way, and can deliver any time of the day or night—so don't be surprised if the litter suddenly appears just when you aren't looking. If you are present during the birth, try to remove any stillbirths that occur: they are common when there are more than three young in the litter, and the adults will often devour the dead young if they are not removed. There are instances of cannabalism of live young among many rodents, but this is not usually found among Cavies. One exception—ear-chewing—is the result of overcrowding.

If you have been raising your Cavies in groups or colonies, the mother and young can rejoin the group after the birth of the litter. Do provide a shoe box ($5'' \times 8'' \times 12''$) where the mother can protect her young. Other females in the colony will help care for them, and other lactating females will even help nurse them. The father usually ignores his offspring, but occasionally an old boar will attack the babies. Should this occur, remove him at once and keep him separated from the young. During periods of excitement (such as feeding time) even the mother will leave the young. To minimize the chances of injury to the litter by adults, exercise extreme caution when approaching the cage during the first days following the birth. During this time you should also refrain from handling the young; a squeeze or fall could injure them badly.

Watching them grow

Baby Cavy should weigh in at $2\frac{1}{2}$ to 4 ounces, with males slightly heavier than females. Those weighing less than two ounces at birth usually fail to survive. The largest young are produced when the litter size is three or less. There is a good reason for this: the female Cavy has only two mammary glands, and if there are more than three young, some will not receive the proper nourishment. In this case you can supplement their diet by feeding them diluted evaporated milk from a dropper, every two to three hours for the first week. Keep soaked alfalfa hay, chopped cabbage and Cavy pellets available.

The newborn Cavy is a Whiz Kid among mammals, born with a complete coat of hair, a full set of teeth and open eyes. Within

When a male is first placed with a female that is ready to be mated, he will circle her, rub up against her, nibble her ear and in other ways show his interest.

an hour after birth the young can be seen running around, and within two or three days they can eat solid food. If it were necessary, in fact, they could even live without attention from the mother. But to be really healthy, a Cavy baby should nurse for at least 20 and even up to 30 days.

The newborn will grow and develop very rapidly. (Mongrel strains show even faster growth rates than inbred strains.) The young should gain about ⅛ ounce a day for the first two months, and should weigh 12 to 14 ounces by the end of this time. The growth rate slows down at this point, and the Cavies reach full maturity—usually around the fifth month—at a weight of 25 ounces for males and 23 ounces for females. They will continue to grow until about the fifteenth month, when females will reach around 28 ounces and males 33 ounces or more. By this time, your first-litter Cavies may be parents themselves—or even grandparents.

Breeding problems

Breeding failure. Infertility may be traced to any of a number of causes. Poor health is one; lack of Vitamin E may be another; age is another cause (fertility slackens off after 30 months); heredity

44

may also play a part (inbreeding sometimes leads to infertility). In general, if you allow young females to develop fully and make sure they are given proper nutrition and care, you'll have no problem.

Premature births. The female may have been bred too young, or may be too fat or too weak. She may suffer from overhandling, overcrowding, damp or dirty quarters, or the scars of fighting. Finally, she may be deficient in Vitamin E. Premature births due to any of these factors can be prevented by proper husbandry.

Stillbirths. These may be traced to individual large fetuses, which cause prolonged or difficult labor (dystocia).

Hereditary defects

Blindness. This is usually the result of inbreeding and is a good indicator that it's time to refresh your breeding stock by using a new boar.

Polydactylism (extra toes). This is also the result of inbreeding. It is usually harmless and can even be used as a genetic "marker."

Inbred specimens usually resemble each other closely.

SALLY ANNE THOMPSON

9   The genetics of Cavy breeding

Genetics is the study of heredity, or how offspring receive their characteristics from their parents. The basic laws of inheritance were first discovered in 1865 by an Austrian monk, Gregor Mendel, who experimented with garden sweet peas. Understanding Mendel's law is indispensable for the breeder, and worthwhile for any pet owner as well; put into everyday terms, it is easy to follow.

Blueprints for heredity

The reproductive cell of the female is called the egg or ovum, that of the male, the sperm. When a sperm penetrates the egg, a new individual is conceived. Each parent contributes half of the new animal's genes. Genes are contained in tiny "packets" linked together like beads on a string. These are called chromosomes: chromosomes are always paired except in the sperm, which has single chromosomes. When the sperm penetrates and fertilizes the egg, the chromosomes in the egg split lengthwise to form a pair. One of the pair clumps up into what is called a polar body and is discarded. The other half matches with the half chromosome of the sperm to create a new individual. In the impregnated ovum, the newly formed chromosome contains the detailed blueprints for the infant's heredity: half from one parent, half from the other.

Mendel's experiment

Mendel noticed that when he crossed tall garden peas with dwarf peas, the offspring were not medium-sized peas as one might suppose, but were all tall. The gene (or blueprint) for Tall had taken precedence over the gene that blueprinted Dwarf. (In genetics, the term for such a gene is *dominant*.) The weaker blueprint for size, Dwarf, receded into the background. It was *recessive*: it was still there, but was overshadowed by its twin.

When he bred the second generation of peas—the ones that looked tall, but came from the cross between the tall and the dwarf parents—he found that three-quarters of the new pea vines were Tall; one out of four was Dwarf. There were still, however, no medium-sized peas in this third generation. Just Tall or Dwarf.

This explains why many times hereditary traits skip a generation. Many naturalists had wondered about this, but no one before Mendel could come up with the answer.

The hybrids

When the Dwarfs of this third generation were bred together, their offspring were all Dwarfs. When the Talls were bred together, however, the expected didn't happen. Some of the Talls produced only Talls, but some produced both Dwarf and Tall. Mendel worked out a mathematical ratio for his results: 25% Dwarf, 75% Tall, *but*—and this was a very important "but"—of that 75%, one third would be pure dominants (produce only Tall); the other two-thirds would look tall, but would carry the recessive Dwarf gene.

Those plants which produced Tall and Dwarf were actually *hybrids*, that is, they carried genes for both Tall and Dwarf. The recessive Dwarf genes were hidden or masked by the dominant Tall. However, when two of these hybrids were crossed, if a sperm with a gene for Dwarf penetrated an egg which was also Dwarf, they produced a Dwarf.

To sum up: when a dominant gene is paired with another dominant gene, the result is pure dominant; when a dominant gene pairs with a recessive gene, the resultant individual resembles the dominant, but carries the recessive; when a recessive pairs with a recessive, the resulting individual is pure recessive. A recessive is always pure; it can never mask a dominant.

Mendel's law and the Cavy

Now let's forget about Mendel's peas and see what happens when we apply his findings to Cavies. To make it even easier, we'll use a diagram.

Let us substitute for the Tall pea, the Black color of the Cavy; and for the Dwarf pea, the complete absence of black color in the Albino Cavy. We know from long experimentation that black is dominant in Cavies, and we'll call it Pure Black (B for short); we'll call the recessive genes that produce the pure white Cavy

Pure Albino (b for short.) What are the possible outcomes if a Pure Black Cavy is mated to a Pure Albino?

Pure Black = BB × Pure Albino = bb (Remember that genes always occur in pairs)

	B	B
b	Bb	Bb
b	Bb	Bb

Each box represents 25% of the offspring

We can easily see from the diagram that all the young will appear Black, but are hybrid for Albino. Now let's mate the offspring together:

Hybrid Black = Bb × Hybrid Black = Bb

	B	b
B	BB	Bb
b	Bb	bb

The offspring will be:
25% Pure Black (BB)
50% Hybrid Black (Bb)
25% Pure Albino (bb)

These exact percentages will probably not appear in one or two litters, but they will average out when many litters have been bred and studied. Nor is it possible to tell which Cavies, for example, are Pure Black and which are Hybrid Black just by looking at them. You should know the animal's ancestry. If you don't and plan to use a Black male as foundation breeding stock, the only way to make sure that he is Pure Black is through a test cross to a Pure Albino female. Then if any of the offspring are white, you'll know that you have a Hybrid.

For serious Cavy breeders, the thrill lies in breeding a perfect color or type—which, by the way, are very rare and valuable. If your aim, like theirs, is to improve a Cavy strain, you should avoid mixing colors and hair types indiscriminately, since this will

When colors and hair types are crossbred indiscriminately, it's impossible to predict just what the youngsters will look like.

just produce a mongrel breed. (Of course, most of us don't take it quite so academically—we can pair off our pets and enjoy the suspense of not really knowing how the offspring will turn out.)

Crossbreeding. When there are two strains of Cavies, each having good qualities, the breeder selects the best from both and crossbreeds the two strains. When the new generation is produced, those offspring with the desired traits are then *inbred*.

Inbreeding. This means interbreeding the same stock without introducing new unrelated individuals. It is used by breeders to create and maintain any pure strain. To be considered pure, a strain must consistently breed the same, such as for color.

To inbreed, you breed the father to his daughter and the son to his mother. Brothers can be bred to sisters but this crossing should be avoided. Inbreeding is not dangerous if selection of animals to use in the future is very rigid. Any that are not up to standard must be ruthlessly discarded. The primary objective is to expose the hidden traits, good or bad.

Line breeding. Here, too, related individuals are mated, but not as closely as in inbreeding. For example, you might mate cousin to cousin or uncle to niece.

Breeding know-how

Regardless of the type of breeding pattern that is used, the key to success is selection—picking out what you think is the best—or, more specifically, selection with a knowledge of genetics. You should only select for breeding those animals that produce off-spring with desired qualities. When the pure strain is achieved, the breeder should use random breeding within the group of selected animals. Just remember, you can only select from those characteristics that are already present in the gene pool from which you are breeding.

Of course, the object of the breeder is to produce a specimen as nearly perfect in all respects as possible, and it would be useless to produce one perfect in color and size but imperfect in shape. In order to avoid this, breeding operations are balanced. If you have a female that is ideal in color and size but somewhat weak in shape, mate her to a male whose outstanding characteristic is his shape—if one lacks a desired characteristic, compensate for it with one of the opposite sex.

To help you with your genetic planning, here is a list of Cavy characteristics in order of relative dominance. (Any color on the list is dominant over all colors found below it.)

Coat color

(Most dominant)	Black
	Brown
	Red
	Golden
	Orange
	Cream
	Lilac
(Least dominant)	White

Coat type

Rosettes and long hair are transmitted by two separate pairs of genes, and neither is dominant over the other. If you breed a pure long-haired Peruvian to a pure rosette-haired Abyssinian, the young will be long-haired with rosettes. But both rosettes and long hair are dominant over short hair.

Spotting is inherited as a separate pair of genes and can be found with any coat type and color. The Himalayan color pattern is a dominantly inherited pattern, and is also controlled by a separate pair of genes, as is the Agouti hair type.

In order to reliably predict the type of offspring you can expect from a cross, you'll need to know how pure the parents are. If you are buying Cavies for breeding experiments, accept only animals with an ancestral breeding record. Usually the purest Cavies—genetically speaking—can be obtained from established breeders: your veterinarian or the American Rabbit Breeders Association (see p. 63) can probably help you get in touch with one in your area.

A quick breeding summary

Breeding season	Anytime
Breeding age (average)	Male: 56 days Female: 68 days
First possible litter	20 weeks
Length of estrus cycle	16–19 days
Duration of estrus	6–11 hours
Gestation	65 to 70 days
Litter size	1 to 9 (average 3)
Birth weight	$2\frac{1}{2}$–$3\frac{1}{3}$ ounces
Eats solid foods	2–3 days
Breeding life	Male: 5 years Female: 4–5 years

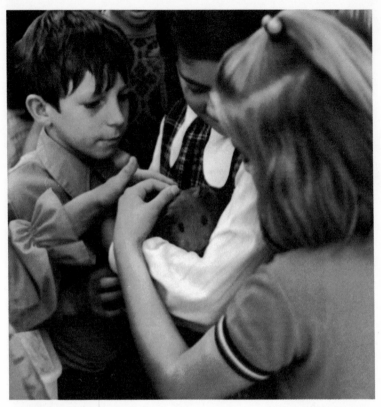

Since Cavies seldom bite, even the very youngest children can share the fun and responsibility of caring for them.

10   The classroom Cavy

Many adults, if pressed to remember their grade school years, will probably recall the fifth-grade classroom where they proudly kept a colony of Cavies (though of course everyone called them guinea pigs then). Indeed, having a living animal to care for in the classroom often made coming to school worthwhile; and teachers know that Cavies are among the easiest animals to keep in class— quiet, easy to feed and keep clean, and hardy enough to be handled by many.

Keep a record of how long it takes each Cavy to learn the maze.

Any of the suggestions given in Chapter 3 may be used for classroom housing. If possible, though, provide a larger housing area so that the entire class can observe the colony. (A large aquarium tank would be ideal.) Routine care and feeding can be scheduled on a rotating basis so that every child has an opportunity to learn how to care for the animals. Since Cavies seldom bite, even when handled roughly, the very youngest children can share the fun and responsibility of caring for them. Close supervision and guidance should be provided, of course, to insure that the Cavies are not mishandled or dropped. If one ever does nip, just treat it as you would any scratch or minor wound, washing with soap and water and then applying a mild antiseptic.

Cavy projects can be fun

Younger children can conduct simple experiments in learning in the classroom, while older students will want to try their hands at breeding or carry out experiments in nutrition—remembering, of course, that the objective of nutritional studies is the development of a more complete diet, never the creation of a deficiency. Whatever the project, Cavies provide a painless way to exercise classroom skills such as accurate observation and measurement, data collection and analysis of data in graphs and charts.

Finally, students of all ages can work on photography projects. The action pictures they take of their charges may be used as part of a school Cavy exhibit, or may be kept in a bound scrapbook, with captions added, as a visual diary of the class's experiences.

Natural habitat

An enjoyable classroom project that is easily set up is the development of a naturalistic environment. Line a large wooden box (3 feet high by 4 feet wide by 5 feet long) with plastic, or paint it with waterproof epoxy paint. Line the bottom with a layer of fine gravel, 2½ to 3 inches in depth, and cover this with a sloping layer of soil. Plant grass seed, and place a number of small flower pots filled with pebbles in the soil at two-foot intervals. When the pots are filled, the water will soak into the soil and water the seeds from the bottom, thus saving the Cavies from the fate of wet feet (and possibly a cold). Be sure to provide the proper lighting as suggested in Chapter 3—it's needed by both the Cavy and the grass. When the grass is well under way, the new tenants can move in.

This natural habitat is a perfect setting in which to observe and photograph the Cavies' breeding patterns, their family life and colony behavior. The environment itself will suggest any number of questions: what are the Cavies' grazing patterns? Do they prefer the top or the bottom of the slope? What happens if a miniature rock cave is provided? The students will undoubtedly think of many other points to pursue.

Constructing a learning maze

The best material to use for a Cavy maze—one of the most popular classroom projects—is heavyweight cardboard. Cut a floor (3 feet by 4 feet) and four outer walls (two pieces 13 inches high by 3 feet 2 inches long, and two pieces 13 inches high by 4 feet 2 inches.) By cutting, partially folding and gluing the wall sections to the base, construct an open box. A number of shorter sections can then be glued to the floor inside to form the maze of pathways. There are basically two types of mazes you can build: the T-maze, in which the passageways cut corners at right angles, and the Y-maze, in which the passageways cut at 45° angles.

Running the maze

Now the fun begins. Place the fresh greens at the "goal" point and the Cavy at a starting point, and station one or two timers with stopwatches to record exactly how long it takes the Cavy to reach the goal. If he seems to have a lot of trouble the first time around, you might help him out with a hint: grind lettuce to extract the juice and dribble it along the path so the Cavy can follow his nose from start to finish. Be sure you have some kind of green reward waiting for him at the end of the maze, and always remove him to his regular quarters to enjoy his prize.

The Cavy should be run through the maze at least twice each day. After a few sessions, he should be able to make a beeline for the finish. Once he has learned the pathway by heart, make several detours in the maze and test to see how much time he needs to learn the new route. Compare the time needed by Cavy

Children handling animals are both students and teachers. They are learning to be gentle but firm, while teaching their charges friendliness and lack of fear.

A, Cavy B and Cavy C for the first maze and for relearning.

Operant conditioning

If the students have decided on a project that involves training the Cavy, they'll want to find out exactly how to go about it. Obviously, one cannot train a Cavy using the same methods as one does when training a dog. They're just not built the same way, and they don't have the same responses.

The best training method is a procedure known as operant conditioning. This involves reinforcing a specific activity which the animal performs. If this is done consistently, after a while he will repeat the action when the signal is given. For example, take away your pet's food for six to eight hours—just long enough for him to get good and hungry. Then, holding a metal cricket or snapper, extend one hand just over his head. He'll look up in expectation of food, and when he does, drop a pellet right in front of him. As he lowers his head to pick up the pellet, snap the cricket and say "Dance!" Keep doing this, and before too long when you give the command "Dance" and snap the cricket, you will find your pet bobbing his head up and down in a beguiling manner. But remember, the cricket must be sounded as he is lowering his head, not after it's completely down, or when it's on the way up. Otherwise he won't learn properly. This type of training calls for patience, practice and good reflexes, but it is very productive.

If you watch your Cavy, you will find that he tends to repeat

Before taking your pet's picture, be sure that he is scrupulously cleaned and groomed. An Abyssinian should have his rosettes carefully brushed into whorls.

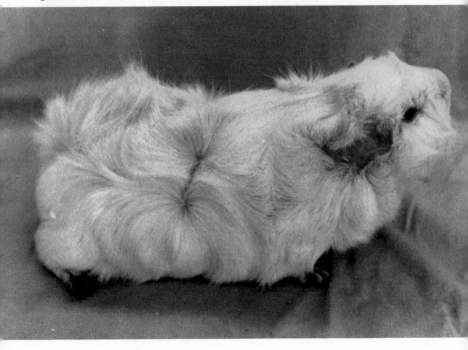

certain actions. By reinforcing these actions with a command, the cricket and food, you can get him to repeat these actions at your request. After a while you can dispense with the reward—the cricket and the command will be sufficient. With a little imagination and observation, you can think of many things to teach your Cavy—to put his front feet up on a block, run around in a circle or nose a small plastic ball around the cage.

Finally, to reproduce a classic operant conditioning experiment, construct a box about two feet square. On one side, cut a small door; be sure you can close this door. Next, place a small pedal inside the box at the foot of the door. Whenever the Cavy puts his front paws on the pedal, give him a small piece of lettuce or carrot through the door, as a reward. He will soon learn to make the connection between his pedal-pushing and the reward. Check his activity with a stopwatch and record the time between responses. Once the Cavy has been conditioned, move the pedal to another spot in the box and repeat the experiment. Needless to say, the Cavy should be left in the box only during the training sessions. (If you would like to purchase an operant conditioning box especially made for Cavies, rather than make one yourself, they are manufactured by a number of scientific supply firms. Ask your public librarian to help you find the address of a firm to contact.)

11 Photographing your Cavy

Someday you may find yourself, just like a proud parent, trying to tell a friend about your exhibit-ripe Peruvian or your new brood of Silver Agoutis. If it isn't possible to show off your pets in person, the next best thing you can do is capture them on film. Cavy photography can be a delightful hobby, and once you've started you'll probably go far beyond that "one picture" you wanted to show your friends.

The formal photo

If the posed portrait is your main interest, you will want to have your pet scrupulously groomed (see Chapter 6) when you send him before the camera. Of course, the most satisfying results will be achieved with color film. Even if your Cavy is solid black or white, color will show him to best advantage, especially if the background is well chosen. An easily constructed background is provided by cloth material, which can be draped over almost anything (try boxes, or "steps" made from a pile of books) to furnish a variety of settings. Shiny material should be avoided, as it may cause over exposure. Be sure to select a background shade that will enhance—not clash with—your Cavy's own color. If your pet is dark brown or black, choose a color such as light blue or beige; pure white would be too great a contrast. If your Cavy is white, cream or lilac, use a darker color, but again, remember that the picture will be spoiled if the contrast is too strong. For best portrait results, a light meter should be used, but perfectly good pictures can be obtained even with a simple camera.

If your pet is used to you and is always handled gently, there should not be any unusual problems in posing him. In fact, one of the Cavy's many wonderful traits is his ability to "stay put" for the camera. One photo buff who spent an afternoon shooting a family of Abyssinians even commented that his human models could learn something about posing from the Cavy!

Candid Cavy

Even more fascinating than portrait photography will be the moving pictures you take of your pet, and you'll find you can photograph him in an almost unlimited number of activities. The majority of your action shots can be taken at the shutter speeds of most inexpensive cameras. If rapid motion is involved, however, you'll need a camera with a faster shutter speed, preferably one with a capability of about 250 frames per second. At this speed you'll be able to "pan" your shots—that is, follow the Cavy's action with the camera while taking the picture. For a really exciting venture, try taking home movies of your Cavy.

As we all know from our experiences with family photography, the secret of successful action shooting lies in taking advantage of the opportunity to catch your subject just being himself. Don't try to force your Cavy to "do" anything special. Instead, pretend you're a photographer on an assignment for Candid Camera, summon up your patience, and keep your hand ready on the

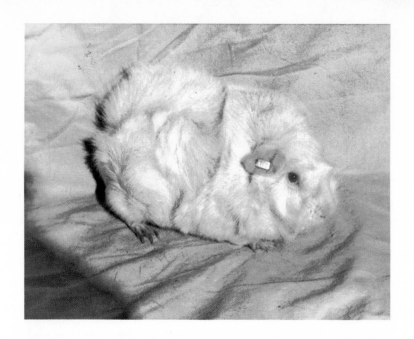

Each Cavy in the show must be marked for identification.

shutter. You may catch your Cavy playing with a favorite toy, munching on a piece of lettuce, or poking his nose wistfully through the wires of the cage. If you have more than one Cavy, the scenes of their social life will fill more than one photo album. Remember, just let your pet "do his own thing," and you'll never be at a loss for top camera material.

12 Showing

A breeder really discovers the quality of his Cavies through exhibiting at pet stock shows. Cash prizes are awarded at many of the larger shows, and many sales can be made in the showroom. Even more important, a breeder may become nationally known if he exhibits high-quality stock.

The smaller local or community shows should not be overlooked either. They bring local breeders and fanciers together, affording the pet owner an excellent opportunity to get acquainted with older breeders and acquire valuable information and new friends.

Getting ready for the show

When you first begin to exhibit, don't hesitate to ask the old-timers for advice. They know all the "tricks of the trade"—that is, the most efficient ways to prepare for a show in conformance with the rules established by the American Rabbit Breeders Association (ARBA).

Needless to say, it is against ARBA show rules to use any "tricks" to modify the physical appearance of the Cavy in any way. Some of the attempts at cheating that have been detected by the expert eyes of ARBA judges have been dyeing the Cavy's hair, using hair spray on the coat, painting shoe polish on the toenails, and removing stray or discolored hairs. When a judge evaluates a Cavy, he is trying to select the best of the best, and any alterations on the part of the exhibitor will result in automatic disqualification.

When you look for exhibition stock, follow the same guidelines you would use in the selection of breeding stock—never choose anything but the most perfect. A few of the most important points considered at exhibitions are listed here; keep them in mind when you select and groom your show Cavy.

1. Type
   a. Round nose
   b. Droopy ears
   c. Bright, prominent eyes
   d. Feet tucked under the body
   e. Round sloping rump
2. Color

True to color as described in Chapter 1. Any deviation from color will restrict the placing of your Cavy.

3. Show grooming
   a. The short-haired American Cavy can be prepared for show in this manner: rub the hair the wrong way, to dislodge loose dirt and unwanted guard hairs. Then rub the Cavy with your

hand; this will smooth the hair down and stimulate the oil glands in the skin.

b. To prepare the Abby for show, all that is required is a good display of the rosettes. A toothbrush can be used to place them properly.

c. The Peruvian is the most difficult to groom, but if you follow the procedures suggested in Chapter 6 you should be well prepared by show day. On the morning of the big day, remove the curlers from the Cavy's hair and thoroughly comb and fluff the hair so that it's no longer possible to tell whether your pet is coming or going.

Classes

When you are ready to show your Cavy, you will enter under one of the following classes:

Junior sow	Female under 22 oz
Junior boar	Male under 22 oz
Intermediate sow	Female between 22 and 30 oz
Intermediate boar	Male between 22 and 30 oz
Senior sow	Female over 30 oz
Senior boar	Male over 30 oz

These six basic classes are then subdivided into the various categories that are selected to make up a show. The categories usually featured at ARBA-sanctioned shows are based on coat type and color. The following hair colors may be included: 1. Self colors: black, white, chocolate, red, beige, cream and lilac; 2. Dutch; 3. Himalayan; 4. Tortoise-and-White. Any of these hair colors may be shown in Cavies with any of the three hair coat types—American, Abyssinian or Peruvian.

In most shows where young breeders are invited to participate, a class known as AOC (Any Other Color) is usually also included, although it is no longer recognized by the ARBA as an official category. This is a catch-all category, providing for any Cavy that does not fit into one of the regular categories. The AOC was devised in order to encourage young breeders, as well as to provide for any new colors which may be developed.

Finally, before you set out for the first exhibition, be sure your Cavy has been trained to sit quietly on a table. He will have to remain immobile while the judge evaluates his qualities in comparison with the other Cavies in the same class.

If the idea of showing interests you, you may want to study the show rules and regulations in more detail. For a copy of the official ARBA book on "Standards of Perfection," write to the American Rabbit Breeders Association at 4323 Murray Avenue, Pittsburgh, Pa. 15217. In fact, if you are serious about breeding or showing Cavies, the best investment you can make is to join the ARBA; they will put you in touch with a local Cavy breeders' club that can furnish information about exhibitions in your area. In England write to:

P. Parkinson, Secretary
National Cavy Club
23 Union Street
Slaithwaite
Nr. Huddersfield Hd7 5Ed
Yorkshire

13 Your aging Cavy

With proper care, the Cavy may live to be over seven years old. If your pet has reached retirement age, try to remember that old animals are very sensitive to any changes in environment and feeding habits. He will require more attention, a quiet corner and the best food. (Of course, his breeding years are long since over.)

Extreme symptoms of old age may cause the Cavy a great deal of distress. As is the case with other aged animals, his hearing may become poor and his eyesight dim. Eventually he may have digestive disorders or kidney malfunction. If you've raised your Cavy from infancy, it is understandable that you have a soft spot for your old friend, but it may be most humane to prevent drawn-out suffering by having him put to sleep. If you find that your aging pet seems to be in pain or discomfort, call on your veterinarian for advice and assistance.

14 Conclusion

Our furry friend the Cavy is gentle, quiet and affectionate, but also hardy enough to spend a lot of time in play activity, or being held and cuddled by some lucky child. Actually, the perfect label for the Cavy might be "For Kids from 6 to 60." Even very young children can learn to care for a Cavy, and so develop a sense of responsibility for another living creature; and this is a friendship that will grow, for with proper attention your pet will be around for a long time. For older children and adults, the joy of Cavy ownership lies in creative breeding—in trying to develop a new strain or color variation. From the sleek perfection of the Self Cavy to the elegant beauty of the Peruvian, there's a Cavy for everyone!

SALLY ANNE THOMPSON

Our furry friend the Cavy is gentle, quiet and affectionate.